QUICK-FIX SCIENCE

# FORCES AND MAGNETS

PAUL MASON

**Meet Snappy.**

Snappy is a young Nile crocodile.

Most crocodiles are only interested in eating and sleeping, but Snappy is different.

Snappy is interested in science, too.

**Please visit our website, www.garethstevens.com. For a free color catalog of all our high-quality books, call toll free 1-800-542-2595 or fax 1-877-542-2596.**

**Cataloging-in-Publication Data**
Names: Mason, Paul.
Title: Forces and magnets / Paul Mason.
Description: Buffalo, NY : Gareth Stevens Publishing, 2026. | Series: Quick-fix science | Includes glossary and index.
Identifiers: ISBN 9781482473872 (pbk.) | ISBN 9781482473889 (library bound) | ISBN 9781482473896 (ebook)
Subjects: LCSH: Force and energy--Juvenile literature. | Magnetism--Juvenile literature.
Classification: LCC QC73.4 M376 2026 | DDC 531.6--dc23

Published in 2026 by
**Gareth Stevens Publishing**
2544 Clinton St.
Buffalo, NY 14224

First published in Great Britain in 2021 by Wayland



**Design:** www.rocketdesign-ltd.co.uk

**Editor:** Nicola Edwards

Cover and interior Snappy artwork by John Haslam

Picture acknowledgements:
Shutterstock: Africa Studio 16cl; Anamuka 29c; Avicon 16c; Aisyah Az Zahra 8-9b; Alex Bard 15cl; Bmszealand 10c; Cy Bo fr cover br, 20bl; Aleksey Boyko 19br; Alexey Broslavets 22tr; Marti Bug Catcher 7b; Marcel Clemens 5tl; Harry Collins Photography 17br; Max Dallocco, elements furnished by NASA 6-7tc, 8bl; Dvande 20br; Dwinsssdy 16tr; Svetlana Foote 27; Four Oaks 6br; grey_and 21cl; Jan Willem van Hofwegen 13tl, 13tr; Hope05 5bl; IvanC7 1, 21b; Akkjarat Jarusilawong 15br; J10 8-9c; Jumi Story 12t; Vladimir Korostyshevskiy 5c; Katerina Krasikova 13bl; Lightitup 24bc; Martine Liu 58 15tr; Lzf 19cr; Masik0553 13bc; Master1305 5tr; Matsabe 8-9c; Milagli 26cr; Milan1983 12b; Captain Milos 15cr; Mipan 3tl, 29t; Dina Morozova 11c; Nerthuz 8br, 9br; Nicku 9t; New Africa 5cr; Nicescene 23tr; Zoran Orcik 5cl; Maryna Osadcha 11t; Chalermpon Poungpeth 13cr; Pozitivo 16b; Quality Stock Arts 22br; Rawf8 22cr; Red Tiger 15bl; Revers f cover tl; Vladimir Rubanov 4b, 10b; Roman Samborskyi 17bl; Slowmotiongli 17bc; snapgalleria 25t; Ody Stocker 22bl; stockyimages 6bc; Suit Stock Photo 23tl; Sunward Art 3tr, 21cr; Taffpixture 7c; Tartila 10cr; Vibrant Image Studio 6cl; Vvoe 26bl; Wasantha 8958 18t; Wavebreakmedia 4c; White vector 17t; Suwat wongkham f cover cr; Carlos Yudica f cover tr; Yuriy2012 18-19c; Zizou7 25b.



Printed in the United States of America

CPSIA compliance information: Batch #CSGS26: For further information contact Gareth Stevens at 1-800-542-2595.

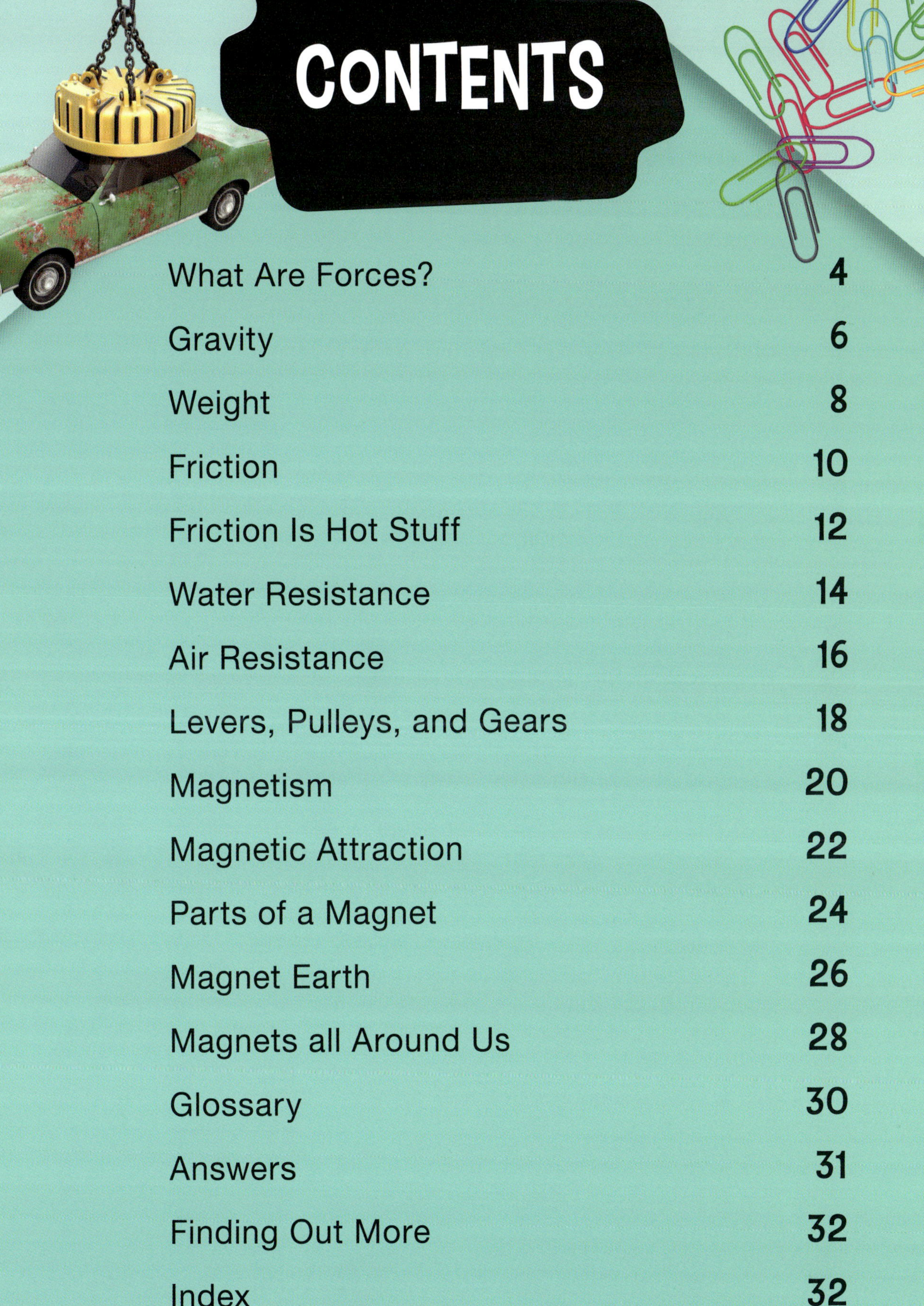

# CONTENTS

# WHAT ARE FORCES?

Forces are pushes and pulls. Look around and you will see that we use them all the time.

To hold onto something that wants to get away, we use pulling force:

Must ... hold ... on.

Mustn't ... fall ... over.

Pull!

Pull!

See if you can work out some of the forces in these photos (Warning: One of them is a joke). Think about air resistance, friction, gravity, and magnetism.

Find out if you were right on page 31.

**1.** **Which force keeps this rock climber's shoes stuck to the rock face?**

To pedal a bicycle or get speed on a skateboard, we use a pushing force.

To cut a slice of bread, people push AND pull on the knife.

**2.** **Which force causes a skydiver to fall? And which force slows them down?**

**3.** **How does this street performer float in the air?**

**4.** **Which force keeps these things stuck on the fridge door?**

# GRAVITY

**This first force is one that's useful for everyone including crocodiles who want to stay in their river ...**

This force is called gravity. It is a pulling force. Here are three top gravity facts:

**In real life there would not be a label on this scene to show you gravity. Gravity would be invisible.**

**1.**

### Gravity Is Invisible

You cannot see gravity. You can only see its effects.

**2.**

### Everything Has Gravity

All objects have gravity, from lightweight insects to tiny pebbles and whole **planets**.

## 3. Gravity Is Not Always the Same Strength

Bigger objects have stronger gravity. The biggest object near us is Earth itself. Earth's gravity pulls objects towards it.



See if you were right on page 31.

# WEIGHT

Some objects are harder to pick up than others because they weigh more. A heavy fish is a good thing, of course! Yum!

Weight is a force caused by gravity's pull. Gravity is stronger on big planets than on small ones. This means a person's weight would be different on other planets:

**If you weighed 88 pounds (40 kg) on Earth (or roughly five dachshunds),**

**... on Mars, you would weigh 33 pounds (15 kg) or as much as two dachshunds,**

**Mars' gravity = 37.2% of Earth's gravity**

## Newtons

Like all forces, weight can be measured in Newtons. Newtons are named after Sir Isaac Newton, the scientist who first described gravity and how it works.

Hair: 0/10

Science genius-ing: 10/10

... on Neptune you would weigh 101 pounds (46 kg) or roughly six dachshunds,

on Jupiter you would weigh 223 pounds (101 kg,) which is 13.5 dachshunds.

Neptune's gravity = 114% of Earth's gravity

Jupiter's gravity = 253.1% of Earth's gravity

# FRICTION

Friction is a pulling force. It happens when one object rubs against another, like when you slide down a dry riverbank.

Whenever an object rubs against something, it produces friction. Rubbing objects together with more force produces more friction.

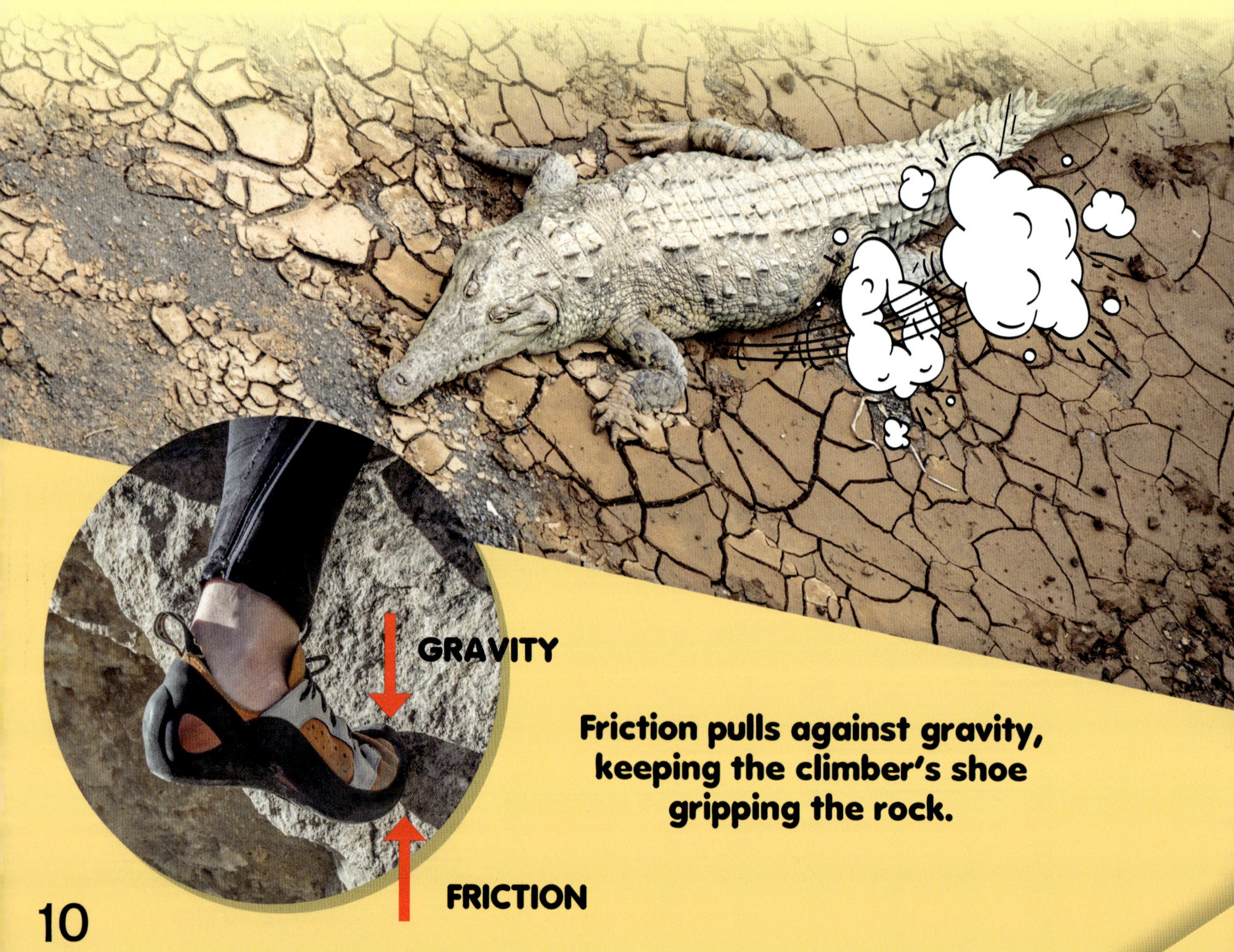


Friction pulls against gravity, keeping the climber's shoe gripping the rock.

## Rough vs. Smooth

Whenever two objects move against each other, they produce friction. If one or both of them has a rough surface, like sandpaper, for example, they produce more friction.

**Using rough sandpaper means you have to push with a lot of force.**

**Pushing ordinary paper across wood needs less force.**

Which would make more friction between the climbing shoe and the rock?

a) a climber weighing 154 pounds (70 kg)

b) a climber weighing 88 pounds (40 kg)

c) both make the same friction

See if you're right on page 31.

# FRICTION IS HOT STUFF

Friction can be a pain. Literally! Friction produces heat ... sometimes it makes enough heat to burn you.

**Friction and You**

Try rubbing your hands lightly together.

Now do the same, but press them together hard.

Do they feel warmer one way than the other?

Friction can be useful if you want to start a fire or grip a surface (like the climber on page 10).

## Fighting Friction

One way to fight friction is to push against it with a bigger force:

**1 x crocodile = less force**

**Amount of friction is the same**

**2 x crocodiles = more force**

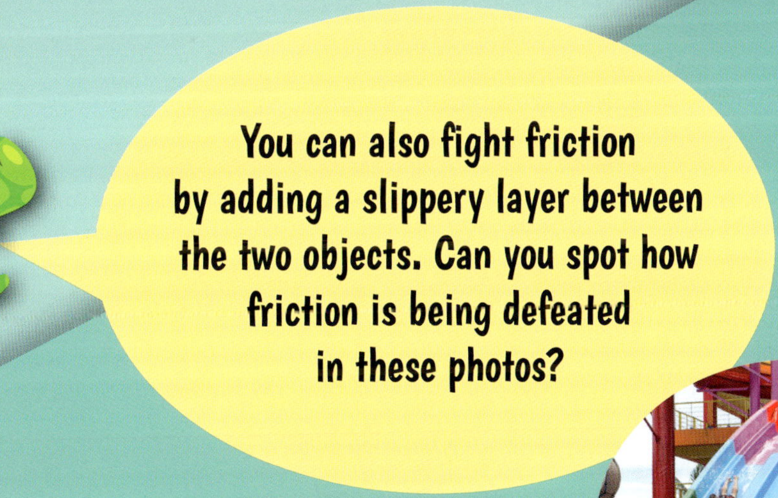

You can also fight friction by adding a slippery layer between the two objects. Can you spot how friction is being defeated in these photos?

Find out if you were right on page 31.

# WATER RESISTANCE

Water resistance is a pulling force. It is the pull of water on objects that are trying to move through it.

Snappy is catching the frightened human because of water resistance. Small objects feel less water resistance than big ones.

## Check Your Water Resistance

Next time you go swimming, trying pushing off from the side of the pool with your arms sticking out from your sides.

After that, push off with your arms stretched out ahead of you, in a more arrow-like shape.

Which gets you further?

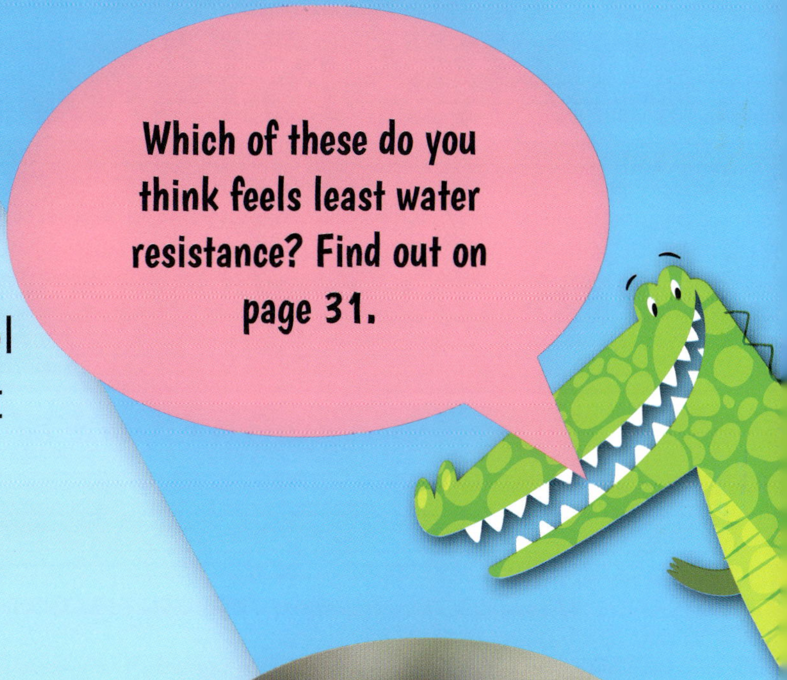

Which of these do you think feels least water resistance? Find out on page 31.

A

kingfisher

B

cannonball

C

elephant swimming

# AIR RESISTANCE

Humans don't move very fast in the water, but they CAN run away quickly on land.

On land, water resistance does not slow you down. Another force, called air resistance, DOES slow you down, but not as much.

### Shape

Imagine trying to cut your food with the wrong side of a knife. It would be much harder than normal. In the same way, an object's shape affects how much air resistance it feels.

Air flow

The supercar feels less air resistance.

Air flows smoothly around the pointy shape of this supercar.

Air flow
Air hits the flat front of the truck and cannot flow smoothly.
The truck feels more air resistance.
Put these living things in order of which would meet the LEAST air resistance. Find out if you were right on page 31.

# PULLEYS, LEVERS, AND GEARS

Have you ever seen a leopard dragging an antelope up a tree? It looks like very hard work! I wonder if it could be made easier ...

Imagine trying to pull an injured climber up a cliff (which is a BIT like pulling an antelope up a tree).

Gnnnnnn!

rescuer

100 pounds (45 kg)

**Pulling them straight up would be impossible:**

Help!

110 pounds (50 kg)

injured climber

**Pulleys** are not the only way to increase force. Here are two other useful ones:

When you have to ride up a steep hill, gears make it much easier.

If you have to move something that does not want to move, a lever makes it easier.

# MAGNETISM

Magnetism is a force that mystified people for thousands of years. (Crocodiles are WAY ahead of you. See how we've been using it for millions of years on page 27).

What is it that makes magnetism so mysterious? It's because magnetism is like other forces in some ways, but different in others:

1. Magnetism can be a push or a pull.

This train is held up by magnetism, which pushes it away from the ground.

These pieces of scrap metal are being lifted by magnetism, which is pulling them upwards.

**2.** Like gravity, magnetism affects objects it does not touch.

Unlike gravity, though, magnetism does not affect ALL objects.

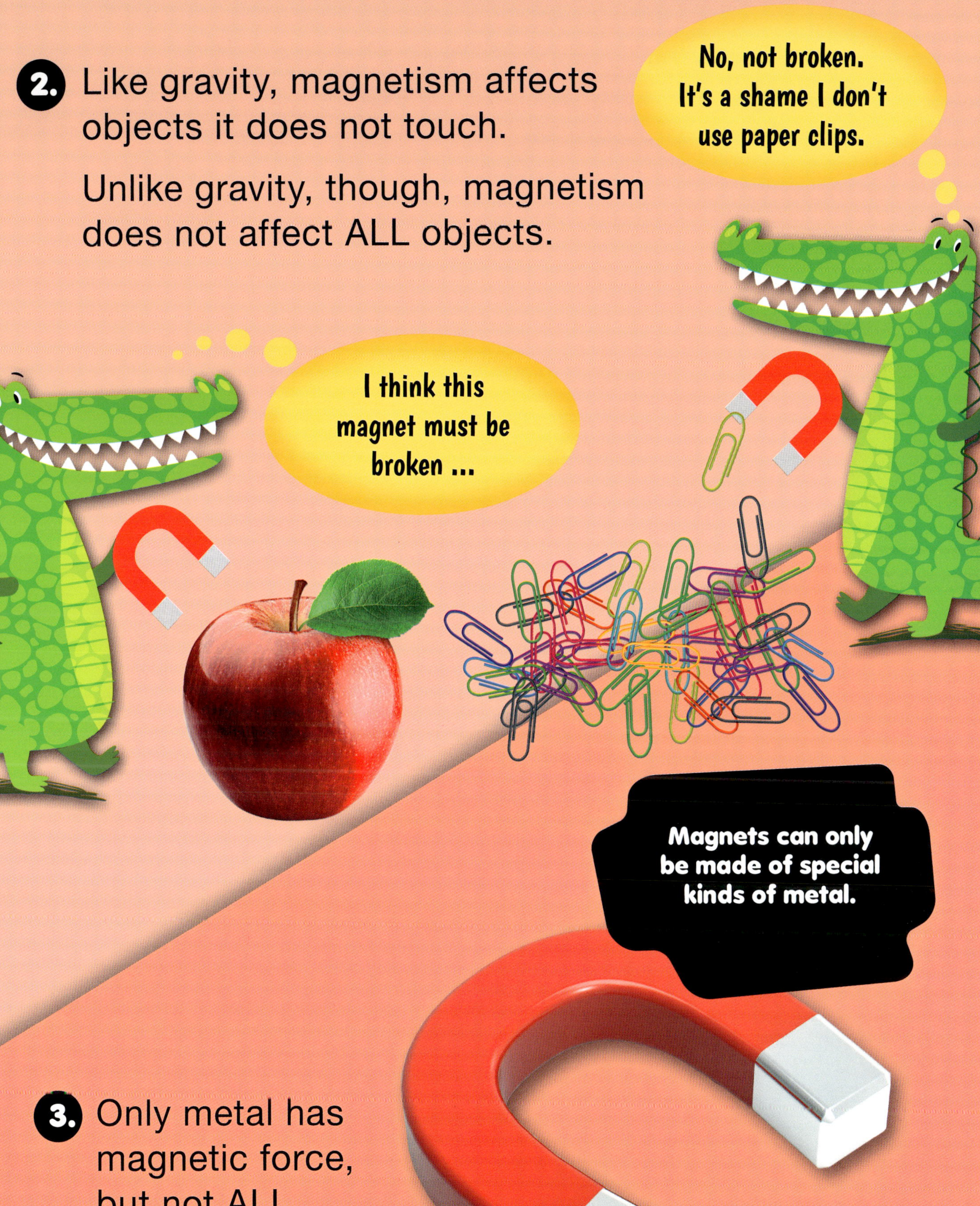


**3.** Only metal has magnetic force, but not ALL metals have it.

# MAGNETIC ATTRACTION

I really can't work out magnetism! My Egypt souvenir magnet just WON'T stick to any of the trees or rocks where I live.

**Magnetism Test**

To help Snappy work out magnetism, you need a magnet, a piece of paper, and a pencil. Walk around and see what the magnet will stick to. Try to test at least 12 different objects. Here are a few ideas to start off with.

Fridge

Brick wall

Car door

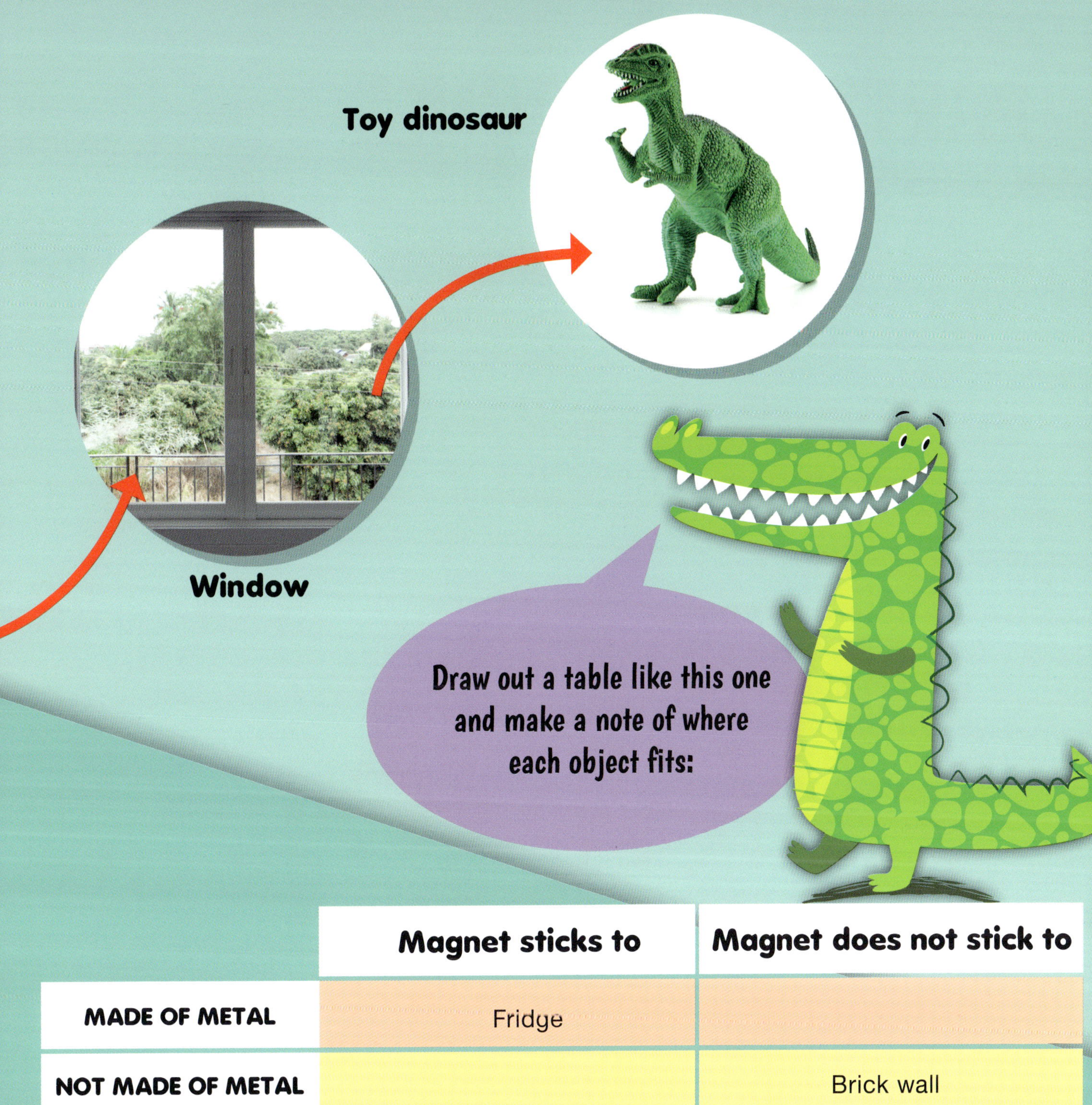


| | Magnet sticks to | Magnet does not stick to |
|---|---|---|
| MADE OF METAL | Fridge | |
| NOT MADE OF METAL | | Brick wall |

The answers will give you some clues about what kind of material feels the force of magnetism. The table will tell you:

1. Are all the "sticks to" objects made of metal?
2. Are all the metal objects also "sticks to" objects?

Check if your table was right on page 31.

# PARTS OF A MAGNET

I wonder what's inside a magnet? They do such amazing things, they must be very complicated inside!

In fact, magnets do not have complicated parts. They ARE different inside, though.

**NON-MAGNET**
**force fields (called "domains") point in different directions.**

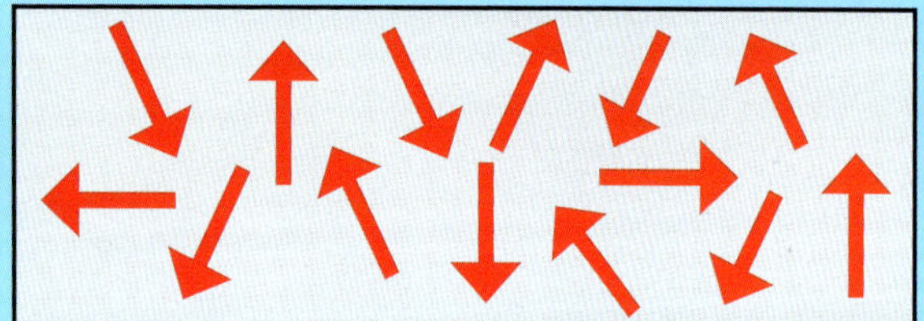

**MAGNET**
**Domains point in same direction**

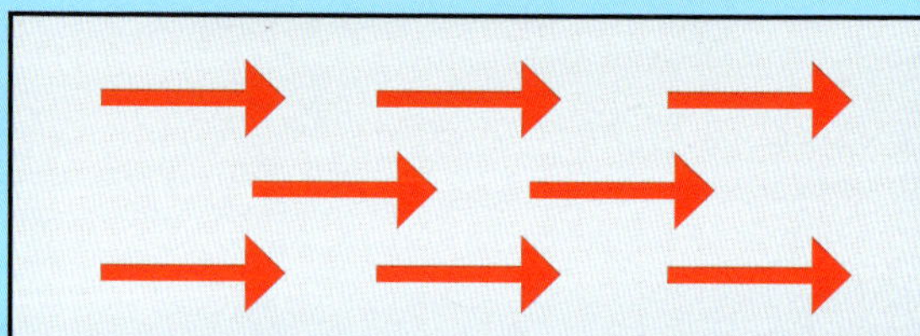

The lined up domains are like this dog team, all pulling in the same direction. They are what give a magnet its force.

## Poles: Pulling and Pushing

Magnets have two ends called the north pole and the south pole. The poles affect how magnets behave toward each other:

- if different poles point at each other, the magnets pull together or **attract**
- if the same poles point at each other, the magnets push away or **repel**.

A magnet's force becomes weaker as it gets further away.

S N

Magnetic field

Will these magnets
a) pull towards each other or
b) push apart?

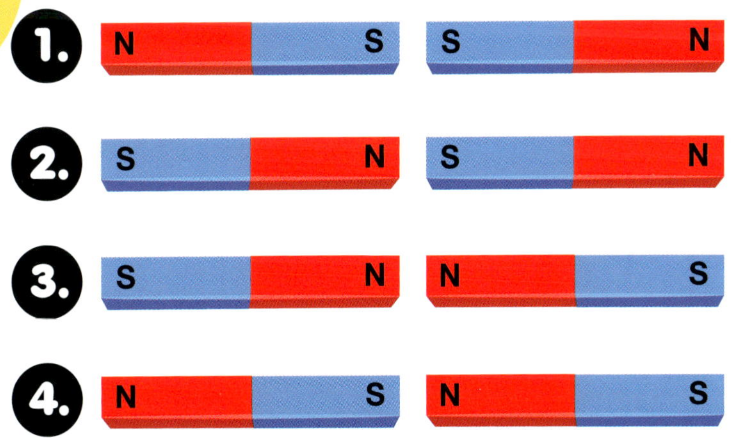


The answers are on page 31.

# MAGNET EARTH

You've probably heard of the North and South Poles (freezing cold places that no self-respecting crocodile would ever visit). Yes, the same names as the ends of a magnet!

Earth itself is a giant magnet. At its **core** is lots of hot metal that is magnetic. It makes a giant version of the magnetic field on page 25.

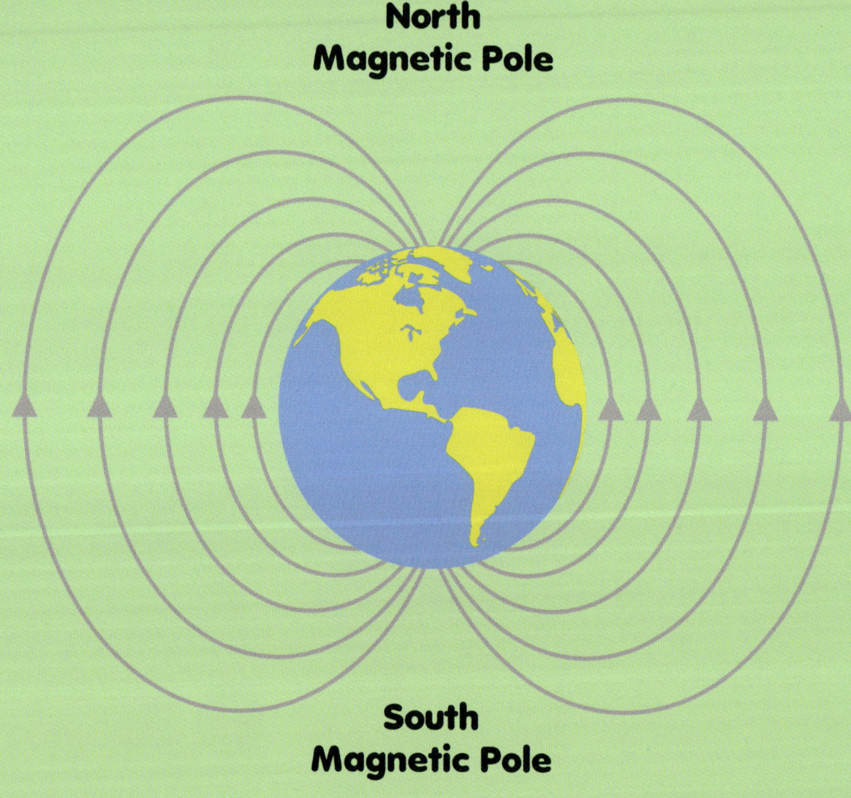

Centuries ago, travelers used magnetic stones to help find their direction. The stones were affected by Earth's magnetism and pointed north or south.

## Animal Magnetism

Scientists think that many animals (including birds, fish, insects, and crocodiles) use Earth's magnetic field to navigate.

Scientists tried using magnets to keep crocodiles away from where people live by using magnets. Here's what they did:

**1. Catch it.**

**2. Tape magnets to the sides of its head.**

**3. Take the crocodile away.**

**4. Remove the magnets before letting it go.**

**The magnets may stop me knowing which way is home.**

# MAGNETS ALL AROUND US

Horseshoes, rings, buttons, and bars ... No, they are not just unusual objects found in vacuum cleaners! They are different kinds of magnet.

### Bar Magnets and Horseshoe Magnets

A magnet is most powerful at its poles. Because bar magnets have narrow poles, they are not very strong.

Horseshoe magnets are bar magnets bent into a horseshoe shape. Because both poles point the same way, these magnets are stronger.

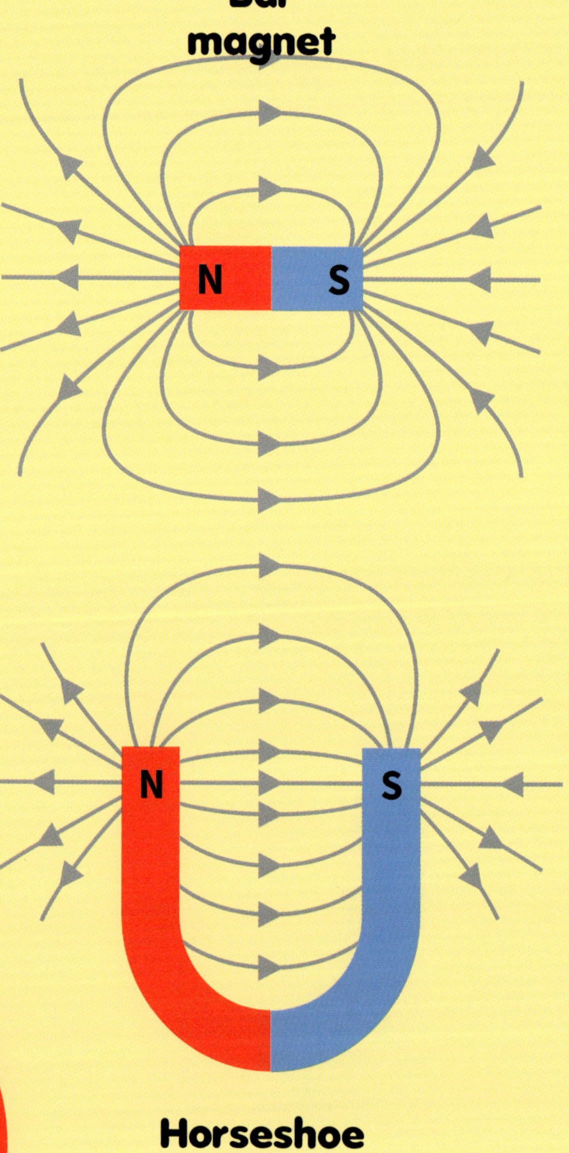


**Horseshoe magnets are a symbol for magnetism all around the world.**

## Button Magnets

The flat ends of button magnets give them a large pole for their size. This makes button magnets strong.

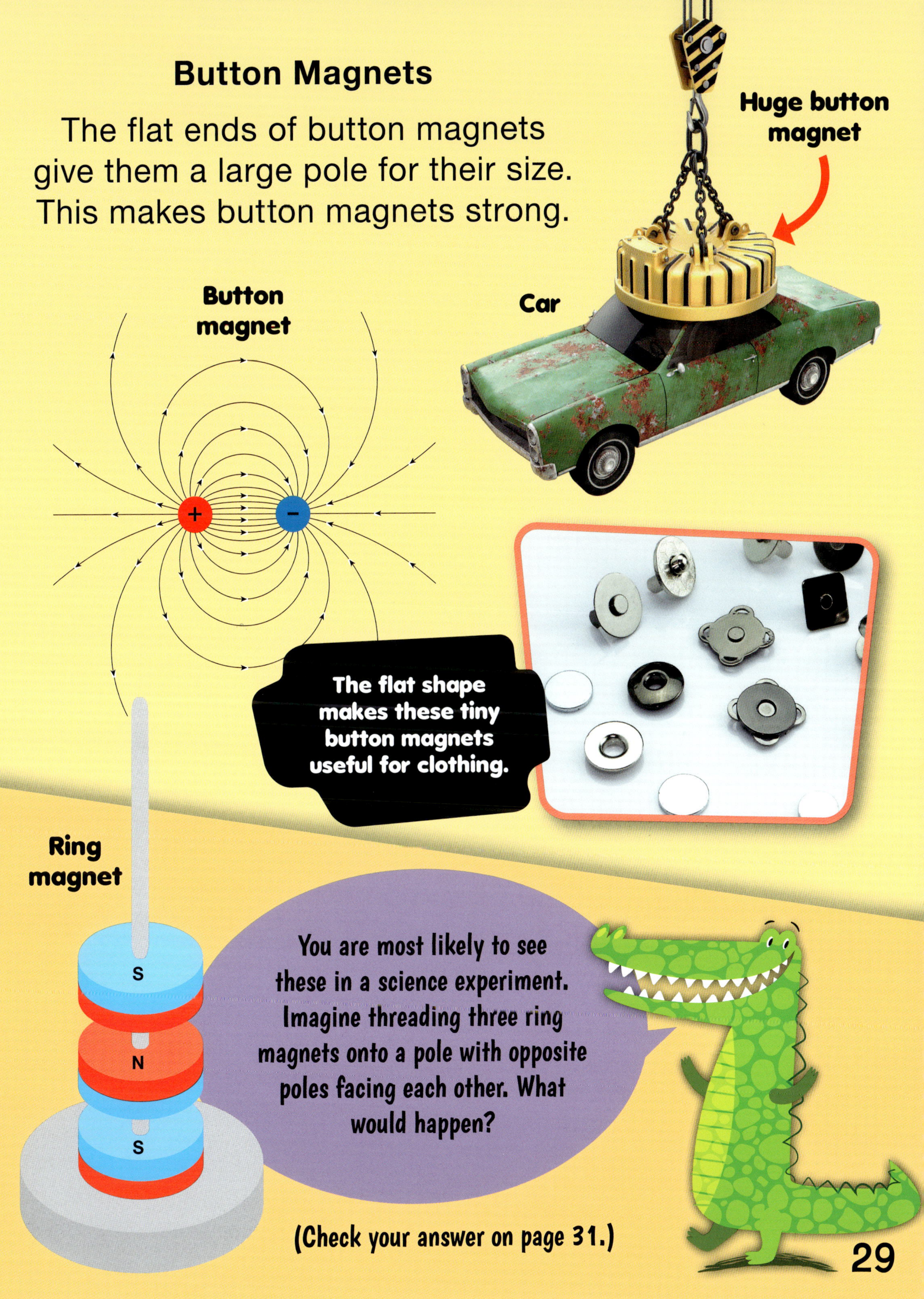


(Check your answer on page 31.)

# GLOSSARY

**attract** pull towards

**core** middle or center of an object (often a round-shaped object)

**domain** tiny area inside an object that has a magnetic field

**force field** an area of energy surrounding an object. Magnets have a magnetic field.

**gears** wheels or discs with teeth on the outside edge. Gears can be used to change the amount of force needed to move an object.

**lever** solid bar resting on a pivot, which can be used to lift or move apart heavy objects

**outline** shape made by the outside edge of an object

**planet** large object in space that moves around a star. Earth is a planet, moving around the Sun (which is a star).

**pulley** something (usually a small wheel with a groove around its edge) that changes the direction in which a rope or cable is traveling

**repel** push away

**skydiver** person that is willing to jump out of an airplane and use a parachute to float to the ground

**symbol** shape that is used to represent something

# ANSWERS

**Page 5**

1 Friction (page 10).

2 Gravity (see page 6) and air resistance (page 16).

3 He doesn't, it's a trick.

4 Magnetism (page 20).

**Page 7**

The pyramid is bigger than Snappy, so it has stronger gravity.

**Page 10/11**

a) The climber who weighs most will make the strongest friction. This is because weight is a force and objects that rub together with more force have more friction.

**Page 13**

The ice skate beats friction using a layer of unfrozen water; the bicycle chain uses oil; the water park slide uses water.

**Page 15**

a) The kingfisher would feel least water resistance, because it is a) small and b) very pointy-shaped.

**Page 17**

1 Peregrine falcons fly up to 200 milles (320 km) per hour

2 Cheetahs run up to 75 miles (120 km) per hour

3 Human world record speed: 27 miles (44 km) per hour.

**Page 23**

1 Yes, everything magnets stick to is made of metal.

2 Not necessarily, because magnets only stick to certain kinds of metal. Usually the metal contains iron, nickel, or cobalt.

**Page 25**

1 S/S: repel

2 N/S: attract

3 N/N: repel

4 S/N: attract

**Page 29**

The magnets would repel each other, so they would hover without touching.

# FINDING OUT MORE

## Books to read

Claybourne, Anna. *Forces.* Tulsa, OK: Kane Miller, 2024.

Lopetz, Christian. *Magnets.* New York, NY: Crabtree Publishing Company, 2022.

Mason, Paul. *Gravity and Other Forces*. London, England, 2024.

## Websites to visit

**wowscience.co.uk**
The sidebar tab for "Forces and magnets" will lead to some fun experiments, which you could do in class or at home with an adult to help.

**spaceplace.nasa.gov/what-is-gravity/en/**
This web page for kids is about gravity. It is from the National Aeronautics and Space Administration (NASA).

**https://www.ducksters.com/science/physics/**
Look under the **Motion** heading to find more information about weight, force, gravity, friction, and more.

# INDEX